# GOODBYE
# GRANDPA

# GOODBYE GRANDPA

## RON KOCH

*Illustrated by*
DON WALLERSTEDT

AUGSBURG PUBLISHING HOUSE
Minneapolis, Minnesota

GOODBYE, GRANDPA

This story is dedicated to some very special people in my life:
to Darlene, and our Joel, Paul, and Jane,
to my mother,
to the people of Bethany and First English,
to my special friends at Green Pine Acres Nursing Home,
and to the memory of my father, Henry Koch,
whose death started me thinking
about a story of this kind.

# CONTENTS

## 1

## BAD NEWS

"Hey Jenn, is mom home from the hospital yet?" Joey Andrews sailed through the door into the back hall of their house.

"Not yet," came the reply from his older sister, Jennifer, who had just finished vacuuming the living room carpet. That was one of her regular Saturday morning duties.

Joey jerked the wet football helmet from his head. He tossed it in the box in the closet off the back hall. "Have you heard anything about how grandpa is?" he asked.

"Nothing," replied Jennifer.

Joey nudged his wet, muddy tennis shoes off without untying them. "Man, were we having a game!" Using his right foot, he steered the soggy shoes on to the rug inside the back door. "Us guys from Oak Street were playing the guys from Phillips Street. We were beating them 42 to 30 when it started raining too much. And they had two junior high guys on their team!"

Standing at the kitchen sink, he gulped down a glass of water. He pushed some damp strands of sand-colored hair from his forehead as he looked out the window at the almost colorless rain falling from a gray, October sky. Using a damp sweatshirt sleeve, he wiped away a few raindrops that were perched on and around the scattering of freckles on his nose.

"I scored three touchdowns and threw a pass to Mike for another one. I intercepted a pass, too." He didn't know if Jennifer was listening to him or not. It really didn't matter.

"Let's play Chinese Checkers," said Joey as he entered the family room.

"Okay," answered Jennifer. "I'm through with everything mom wanted me to do."

They plopped themselves down on the family room carpet. Joey became very serious as he got the marbles ready. He usually wasn't that way. "You know something, Jenn, I'm really scared something bad is going to happen to Grandpa Lane."

Jennifer usually thought more and spoke less than her younger brother. She nodded. She shared his fears. "You can start," she said.

"I think mom is worried, too." Joey was talking while he played. "She started to cry when she

called Uncle Jeff last week to tell him she had taken grandpa to the hospital. Before she left for the hospital this morning, she said that she couldn't sleep last night. She said she kept thinking about grandpa's operation this morning."

They played in silence for awhile. Then Joey asked, "What would we do if grandpa died?"

"Don't even talk that way, Joey," said his sister.

But Joey didn't stop. "He was so sick when they took him to the hospital. And I'm sure Dr. Berry wouldn't want to operate unless something is really wrong. Just think," he continued, "Grandpa Lane has lived with us ever since grandma died. That was about six years ago. We need him. Mom needs him."

Jennifer didn't say a word. She kept playing, pretending she was really concentrating on the game.

Joey had never known his dad. When he was just a baby, his mother and father had many problems. They got a divorce, and Joey's dad moved away from Forestburg. He never came back.

"Maybe grandpa will still be okay," concluded Joey. "Let's just play."

They played in silence for some time. A sly smile crossed Jennifer's face. "I'm going to beat you by at least four moves," she said.

Joey noticed that the braces on her upper teeth

were visible when she smiled so victoriously. He didn't like that. "You're just lucky!" he replied. "I will bet I win as many games as you do, even if you are in junior high now."

"That's silly," said Jennifer.

"Why?" asked Joey.

"When we played last Sunday afternoon, I beat you four games in a row," she answered. "Remember?"

"You were lucky then, too," Joey said. "I was watching the football game on television while we played. I wasn't really trying."

Disgustedly, Jennifer shook her head from side to side. Her long, blond pony tail swished as she turned her head. "You won't admit that I am better than you." She waited for her brother to answer. He didn't.

"You can start this time, too, if you want," said Jennifer. She was turning the board around so the red marbles were in front of Joey again. She had the green ones.

"Aw, let's forget about this silly game," suggested Joey. He did not like losing. "Let's just watch TV." He didn't wait for a word from his sister. Joey scooped the marbles from the board. He dropped them into the marble box one-by-one.

"Hey, there's mom!" exclaimed Jennifer. "I just heard the car door slam." Jumping up from the floor, she ran to the door to the garage. Joey hurriedly finished putting the game back in the cabinet next to the television.

Joey had a question as soon as his mother and Jennifer came into the family room. "Is the operation over?" He didn't give her a chance to answer. Instead, he blurted out another question. "How's grandpa?"

Karen Andrews did not answer her son right away. Slowly she dropped herself into the big recliner chair. She leaned her head against the high back of the recliner and silently looked at the raindrops that were bouncing off the family-room window. Then Joey saw the tears in his mother's eyes.

"Isn't grandpa all right?" Joey asked.

"Oh Joey, Jenn," she said slowly. She paused. Then she said it. "I'm afraid grandpa is going to die." She started to cry.

Quietly Joey and Jennifer sat down on the sofa. They didn't say a word or make a sound. Joey looked at his sister. They did not know what to do when their mother started crying.

Suddenly Joey realized he was about to cry too. He didn't want that to happen. "You mean we will never get to see grandpa again?" he asked quietly. There were tears in his eyes, but he did not cry. Jennifer sat there—as still as a statue.

Mrs. Andrews wiped her eyes with a Kleenex. "You will be able to see grandpa again," she replied. "You see . . ." She paused again to wipe away a few more tears and to blow her nose. She started again. "Dr. Berry told me that grandpa will probably live for several months. He might even be able to come and live at home. At least for a while."

Joey wanted to know more. "What's the matter with grandpa?" he asked. "Why didn't Dr. Berry fix what's wrong with him when he operated?"

Joey and Jennifer sat quietly as their mother explained. "Well, you know that grandpa has not felt well for several weeks. When I took him to see Dr. Berry last week, the doctor was concerned that there was something seriously wrong. That's why we had to put grandpa in the hospital." Her tears were stopped now.

She continued. "The doctor thought that grandpa had cancer. He had to operate to see if that is what it was for sure. He also planned to try to remove the tumor, if that was the problem. But when they operated this morning, they discovered that the cancer had spread so far that they could not even begin to remove it. There was just nothing they could do." She slowly shook her head in sadness as the tears came again.

Joey had more questions, but he didn't ask them.

Finally, Jennifer spoke for the first time. "Mom, you shouldn't cry."

"I'm sorry, sweetheart," answered Mrs. Andrews. "I'm just so sad that I have to cry."

Now Joey sat back in silence as his sister spoke again. "But you know what Pastor Don says. He says that God will always take care of those who love him." Trying to cheer her mother up, Jennifer continued. "We talked about dying just a couple of weeks ago in Sunday school. And our teacher, Mr. Lansing, said that whoever believes in Jesus will live with him forever." Almost excitedly she added, "And you know that grandpa believes and trusts in Jesus!"

Through tears, Karen Andrews smiled at her daughter. "I know that, Jenn. It's just that I am going to miss your grandfather. We all love him so much."

Joey knew how much he would miss Grandpa Lane. So did Jennifer. No one spoke. The only sound was the drumming of the rain against the window. Joey heard Jennifer sniff quietly as she started to cry. Fighting to hold back his own tears, Joey went and stood beside his mother. He put his arm around her. "I love you, mom," he said.

She smiled at him through tear-reddened eyes. "Thank you," she whispered.

"But I'm afraid," admitted Joey. "I don't want grandpa to have to die."

"Come on now, Joey," she said. "You are my

big boy. I didn't think you were ever afraid of anything."

Joey knew he was usually very brave. At least that is what people thought. But now he was afraid. He felt himself getting angry. He really didn't know who he was getting mad at. "I'm sorry," he said, "but Grandpa Lane has to be with us!"

Joey was fighting back tears. His voice got louder. "What can I do?" He got even louder. "I don't like people to be sick! I'm afraid to have grandpa dying! I don't like death! I'm afraid of sickness and death!" he shouted.

Pulling quickly away from his mother, Joey turned and ran up the stairs toward his room.

"Please come back, Joey," his mother called after him. She listened for an answer. But all she heard was crying and the thumping of the cold October rain as it hit against the house on Oak Street.

## 2

# THE VISIT

"Try a post pattern on three." Joey Andrews was calling plays in a two-man huddle. Joey and Mike Tyler both clapped their hands once and moved into their positions. No one was playing against them. They were practicing pass plays.

Mike, Joey's number-one friend, jogged out to the right. He bent down in a football stance. He leaned forward, bracing his right hand against the chilly ground.

Joey hunched over like a quarterback. His hands were reaching under a pretend center. He gripped the football between his hands.

"Ready! Set!" Joey was shouting. "One, two, three." On three, Joey suddenly straightened up and darted back to throw a pass. At the same time, Mike raced straight down the field, which was the Andrews' backyard. Suddenly, Mike slanted toward the left. Joey knew exactly where

Mike was going. He fired the football toward him. The hard spiral whacked into Mike's ribs as he closed his arms around the ball.

"Ow! That one really stung," said Mike. The cold of this November afternoon made the football feel like a rock.

"Good grab," shouted Joey, as his receiver trotted back toward him. "That's the way to be!" he added.

Joey lifted up the face guard on his helmet and spit on the grass, which was now brown. He had seen quarterbacks on TV do that as they got ready to call another play.

"What are you practicing for, the Super Bowl?" Joey looked up and saw his mother walking toward them. He had not seen her drive into the driveway. She said, "It's so cold out here. I thought you two must be practicing for the Vikings or Packers."

Joey smiled. "What are you doing home?" he asked. "I mean, it isn't five yet, is it?"

"No," she said. "It is just a little after four. I got off work early so I can go to the nursing home. They moved Grandpa Lane there. Dr. Berry decided he would have to be in a place like that where there are nurses. They took grandpa there in an ambulance at about noon today." She added, "I have a meeting tonight so I want to visit grandpa before dinner. It's been about three weeks since you've seen grandpa. I thought you might want to go with me to visit him." Joey and Jennifer had been too young to get into the Forestburg Hospital to visit Grandpa Lane there.

"Mom, I'm not sure I want to go to the nursing home. At least not today." Joey was looking for excuses. "I've got a lot to do today."

His mother said, "Maybe we had better talk about that a little. Is Jenn in the house?"

His nod indicated that she was.

Joey's mother spoke again. "Mike, you probably should go home now. We have to go in the house and talk about Grandpa Lane."

"See ya," Mike said and trotted toward his house, just across the street.

As Joey and his mother neared the house, they could hear Jennifer practicing the piano. Chipper, their little beagle, barked as they opened the door.

"Brrr. It's cold out there." Mrs. Andrews pretended to shiver as she pulled off her coat and draped it over the back of a chair.

"What are you doing at home?" Jennifer came with the same question Joey had asked. Their mother retold the news that Grandpa Lane had been taken to the Forest View Nursing Home.

"Now," she concluded, "I want Joey to put his school clothes back on. We will all go and visit grandpa before we eat."

Joey spoke very quietly. "Mom, I really don't think I can go along." He had thought a lot about Grandpa Lane's illness in the two weeks since the operation. But, he had said very little about it to his mother.

"Can't go along?" Karen Andrews was surprised at her son's words. "I thought you would be anxious to see your grandfather."

"I do want to see him," said Joey. "But . . . but . . . I've got quite a bit of homework to do. And I haven't practiced piano yet today."

"Come on now, Joey," said his mother. "Usually I have to remind you to do your homework. I have to beg you to practice the piano most of the time. Now be honest. Why don't you want to go along?" She was concerned about her son.

"I'm sorry, mom," Joey mumbled, "but I just don't want to go along. I don't feel like it." He spoke honestly. "I don't know if I want to see grandpa if he is all sick and in bed. And besides that, Todd Ellis went to the nursing home once. He said so many of the people were really sick. Some were all mixed up and acted so goofy. I don't like that, mom."

Joey saw real understanding in his mother's gentle smile. He was almost pleading as he added, "I just don't want to go along."

"I can see why you feel as you do, Joey," she said. "But I know grandpa would really love to see both of you. You know that you two are the most special people in the world for grandpa."

"I know," answered Joey, "but I just don't want to go now. "Why don't you and Jenn go? I'll go along next time."

"Joey," his mother was speaking more firmly now. "I want you to go with us. We won't stay very long."

"But, mom . . ."

"You are going along!" She didn't give him a chance to finish what he wanted to say. "Maybe this will be the best thing for you." She paused for a few seconds. "I won't force you to go along in the future. But today you are going with us."

Joey wanted to say more. He wanted her to understand more about how he felt, but he realized that her mind was made up.

"Now go up to your room. Get your school clothes back on," his mother said.

Joey didn't answer her. He changed his clothes.

Joey wasn't happy as they drove toward the east edge of town and the Forest View Nursing Home.

Karen Andrews saw the worried look on her son's face. She said, "Don't worry, the people at the nursing home aren't all like the ones Todd told you about. Many of the people are just old and have to have special care. Some are a little confused. But not too many."

Joey wasn't talking. She continued, "You know that I have been at the hospital every day since the operation. Grandpa's mind is good. Dr. Berry thinks that he will be able to be up and around before very long. It's no problem to talk to grandpa."

Then Joey spoke. He was pouting. "I just think it is going to be hard to talk to grandpa when he is probably going to die soon."

"Well, we aren't going to talk to him about that!" said Jennifer quickly. "We can talk about other things."

Joey defended what he had said. "I know that. I mean it just won't seem right talking to him knowing that he is dying. It will make me feel creepy."

Jennifer didn't want to talk about that. "By the way, mom," she asked, "does grandpa know that he probably won't get well?"

"Yes," was the answer. "Dr. Berry told him that he won't recover. He had a long talk with him about it a couple of days after the operation."

"What did grandpa say when the doctor told him?" asked Jennifer.

"I guess he told the doctor he expected that," answered Mrs. Andrews. "Grandpa and I haven't talked about it. But I think it has upset him quite a lot."

"I still think grandpa is going to get well."

Joey's ears perked up as Jennifer spoke. "Our whole Sunday school class is praying to God to heal grandpa. So are all my good friends!" Then she added a question, "God does answer prayers, doesn't he?"

Karen Andrews remained silent for several seconds. She turned the car on to the long driveway that led to the Forest View Nursing Home. Then she spoke. "God does answer all of our prayers. I pray for grandpa many times each day. But," she added, "sometimes he answers our prayers in different ways. He doesn't always answer them the way we want them answered."

She drove into a parking space in front of the large, one-story brick building with many windows. The nursing home stood at the edge of the forest which wrapped almost all of the way around Forestburg. "Let's keep praying," she said as she turned off the car. "Maybe something special will happen."

As they walked through the main entry, Mrs. Andrews told her children that this was home for over a hundred people. They walked across the large lobby to the information desk. Joey noticed a number of people from the home were sitting in the big easy chairs in the lobby. Some were talking. A few sat in silence. Two were sleeping.

Joey suddenly felt more like a bashful four-year-old than the usual brave, noisy eleven-year-old that he was. He stayed very close to his mother as she asked which room Grandpa Lane was in.

"Mr. Lane is in Room 127," came the reply. "It is at the end of that hallway, on the left side." The woman at the desk pointed down the long hall to their right.

Jennifer, Joey, and their mother walked down the hall toward Room 127. *This place isn't as bad as I expected,* Joey thought. The doors of most of the rooms were open. Joey noticed that there were two beds in each room. Looking in to the different rooms, he saw that some people were taking naps. A few people were reading. Some were visiting with their roommates or with visitors. Others sat looking out the window or toward the door in silence. *Most of them just look like friendly old people,* he thought. *But some do look awfully sick.*

As they walked into Room 127, Joey saw Grandpa Lane lying in the bed nearest the door. Joey was surprised and hardly recognized his grandfather. Grandpa Lane had been a strong, husky carpenter. He looked so much weaker and thinner than before. Grandpa had always kept his gray, almost white, hair short and neatly combed. Now it looked so much longer, and it was not combed at all.

Grandpa Lane was sleeping. His hands were folded across the front of his blue and white

pajamas. "He looks so pale, so white," Joey whispered to Jennifer.

They both stayed at the doorway. A curtain was pulled between grandpa's bed and the one nearest the windows. The only sound in the room was the loud breathing of the person on the other side of the curtain.

"Dad," Karen Andrews was gently shaking her father.

"Oh!" He seemed surprised to see her. "Hello, Karen."

Joey thought his voice seemed weak, too. Grandpa cleared his throat a couple of times.

His daughter spoke quietly. "I've brought someone special to see you, dad."

Jennifer and Joey stepped closer to the bed.

Grandpa smiled a big smile. "Hi, Jenny," he said. He was the only person who called her Jenny. "Hi, pal." Joey had forgotten that grandpa usually called him that.

Together they answered, "Hi, grandpa."

His broad smile stayed as he reached out and took Jennifer's hand. Then he gripped Joey's hand. "How are my two special pals?" he asked. "I haven't seen you two for a long time."

Again they answered together. "Good."

"I'm afraid I am a little tired today," grandpa said. "The trip over here from the hospital played me out."

Joey remembered how grandpa had always been able to work for hours without getting tired. He felt sad to see grandpa so weak and tired now.

For about ten minutes Jennifer and Joey told grandpa all the latest news. They talked about school and about their friends. Joey told about football. Jennifer talked about cheerleading. They told about the new family that moved in just three doors down. They even told him that Chipper had run away for a couple of days. Whenever they ran out of things to say, their mother would suggest things for them to tell grandpa about. Grandpa Lane said very little. He seemed to enjoy just listening to his two grandchildren. He smiled at them often. His eyes looked very tired though.

Turning to his daughter, grandpa said, "Karen, do you remember George Cooper? He used to run Cooper's Drug Store when you were young."

She remembered him.

"He's on the other side of the curtain," said grandpa. "I guess he has been here for almost ten years. He's real bad. He doesn't know anyone. They don't think he will last long. He is ninety now."

Joey peeked around the curtain as his mother and Grandpa Lane talked about the Cooper family. What Joey saw upset him! Mr. Cooper lay flat on his back. Joey noticed that his mouth was open wide. His eyes were partly open and staring at the ceiling. A kind of quiet rumbling, gurgling sound came from his throat. Joey quickly looked away. He didn't feel very good.

Joey said nothing for a couple of minutes. Grandpa noticed the unusual silence. "What's the matter, pal?" he asked. "What are you thinking about?"

Joey had always been able to talk honestly with grandpa. He spoke honestly now. "I just looked at Mr. Cooper. He looks so bad." Then he added, "I was wondering what you think about death, grandpa."

The smile on grandpa's face was suddenly gone. His answer was quiet, but firm. "I don't want to talk about that!" Tears came to grandpa's eyes. He looked very sad, almost angry.

"I'm sorry, grandpa," said Joey. "I was just wondering . . ." He didn't say anymore. He was mad at himself for asking such a stupid question.

The room became silent. The only sound again was the heavy breathing of Mr. Cooper. Joey's mother broke the silence. She looked at her watch and said, "Oh my, it is almost 5:15. They will probably be bringing your supper soon, dad. We better be going."

Grandpa agreed, admitting that he was getting very tired.

"We will be back tomorrow or the next day," said Mrs. Andrews.

"That will be good," answered grandpa.

"I'll see you, grandpa," said Jennifer.

The sad Joey only said, "Goodbye."

"Thanks for coming," said grandpa. But he seemed so sad and unhappy now. Joey's question about death had upset him.

As Joey turned to leave, he saw his mother bend over the bed and give her father a kiss. "I love you, dad," she said.

"Thank you," he whispered as they left the room.

The three had just started back toward the lobby when Mrs. Andrews stopped by a woman sitting in a wheelchair in the hall. "Hello, Mrs. Simon," she said. "Do you remember me?"

The elderly woman looked at Mrs. Andrews. She did not seem to know her.

Realizing that, Mrs. Andrews added, "I was Karen Lane. I was in your typing class when I was in the tenth grade."

"Karen? Of course I remember you," replied Mrs. Simon. "You will have to pardon me, but I don't see well. I didn't recognize your face." Seeing Jennifer and Joey, she asked, "Are these your children?"

"Yes they are," answered their mom. "This is

Jennifer, and this is Joey." Turning to her children, she added, "I want you to meet Mrs. Simon."

They both said, "Hello."

Joey was not at all happy when he saw that Mrs. Simon wanted to talk to his mother and ask her some questions. He was sad. He didn't feel good. He wanted to get out of that place right away.

When Joey had a chance to speak, he said, "I'll wait in the car, mom." He started toward the lobby without waiting for a word from his mother. He was nearing the lobby when he noticed a woman standing just outside of her room. She was not at all neat. Her grayish-brown hair was uncombed. She stared at Joey as he came near the place where she was standing. She made him nervous.

As he was walking past her room, the woman reached out and touched Joey's arm. She gently grabbed the sleeve of his jacket. Joey felt a sudden fear and a weakness in his knees. Quickly, he jerked his arm free and ran through the lobby. He raced out the door and back to the car. He was crying when he reached the car.

"I'll never go back in there again." Jumping into the back seat of the car, he said it over and over again. "I'll never go back in there again. I'll never go back in there again."

Soon Mrs. Andrews and Jennifer were in the

car. The sun was setting and darkness was settling over Forestburg as they drove. Everyone in the car was quiet.

Then Jennifer spoke. "Grandpa was so different today. He is usually so funny. I don't like it when he is this way." She thought for a short time and then added, "He didn't say a thing about the days on the farm when he was young, or anything like that. I never even thought grandpa looked like an old person before," she observed, "but now he does."

Joey agreed with everything Jennifer said, but he remained silent.

"You are so quiet, Joey," said his mother. "Is anything wrong?" She had not seen what happened with that woman near the lobby.

He mumbled an answer to her question. "Not really."

"What's the matter, Joey?" she asked.

But her son said nothing. He just kept thinking, *I'll never go back to that place again, even if Grandpa Lane is there.*

## 3

# THE SHED

Joey was thinking as he put the milk carton back in the refrigerator. *I have got to think of a way to get out of going along.* He quietly took a small handful of chocolate-chip cookies from the cookie jar. He sat down on a stool near the kitchen window. He had to do more thinking.

It was the day of Christmas Eve. Joey could hear the humming and singing of his sister as she wrapped Christmas presents in the family room. Joey was so busy thinking he hardly heard the doorbell ring.

"Mike is here." Jennifer was calling her brother to the front door.

"Okay," said Joey. "I'm coming."

The Christmas tree looked bright and cheerful as Joey went to the front door. Joey didn't feel that way though.

"Hi, Mike," he said. "What are you up to?"

"Want to come out and help build a snow fort?" Mike asked. "We've got plenty of snow now." Snow had been falling gently all day. It looked like wet cotton as it covered the ground and clung to the trees and bushes.

"I'd like to come out," Joey answered, "but I'm going to the nursing home to visit my grandpa this afternoon."

Mike said, "I didn't think you went down there with Jenn and your mom."

"I've only gone once," said Joey. "That was when grandpa first moved there about six weeks ago." He added gloomily, "Mom says I have to go along today. We have to take our Christmas presents to grandpa."

"Why don't you come out for a while anyway?" asked Mike. "Your mom won't be home for a couple of hours."

"I can't," Joey replied. "They are closing the office mom works at early because of Christmas Eve. She is getting off at three o'clock. We are going to the nursing home just as soon as she gets home."

"How about tomorrow, then?" asked Mike. "Are you going to be able to play then?"

"I think so," answered Joey. "My Uncle Jeff and his wife are coming late this afternoon to spend Christmas with us and with grandpa. I should have some time to come out though."

"Good," said Mike. "See you tomorrow."

"Okay," said Joey. "See you."

"I'll wrap your present for grandpa if you want me to," volunteered Jennifer as Joey closed the door.

"No," he answered. "I'll try to do it myself."

He glanced at the kitchen clock as he went back to his milk and cookies. *It's quarter to three.* He was doing more thinking. *I just can't go along. That place scares me too much. It makes me feel creepy. That old woman who grabbed me might be standing there again. I don't ever want to see her again.*

Jennifer called from the living room again. "Joey, you have got to get your present wrapped. Mom will be home in just a few minutes."

"I know," Joey moaned. He didn't move from the stool though.

*I wonder what would happen if I tried to hide,* pondered Joey. *If mom can't find me, she can't take me along.* He munched on a cookie and sipped some milk. He made a decision. *I've got to disappear for a little while. Then mom can't make me go along.*

*Where can I go?* he wondered. *If I go over to Mike's house, mom will find me right away.*

He finished the last cookie and gulped down the last of the milk. Then he saw it! The shed. The shed was a small wooden building that

Grandpa Lane was building at the back of their lot. He had only finished the outside of it when he got sick. It was to be used for storing the lawn mower and grandpa's tools. Grandpa also had plans to use it as a workshop. He had not put anything in it yet.

Joey stared at the shed, as it stood amidst the falling snowflakes. He thought, *Why not go there? Mom will never look for me in the shed.*

"Please come and wrap your present." Jennifer was calling again. "You know mom wants us to be all ready to go when she gets home. Joey, don't make mom mad!"

"I will be there in just a minute, Jenn," answered Joey. But he was not going toward the family room. Rather, he quietly tiptoed to the back hall. He pulled on his coat. It was still damp from the snowball fight he had been in that morning.

The key for the padlock grandpa had put on the shed door hung on a nail in the closet in the hall. Silently, he slipped the key off the nail. He eased the back door open. Without making a sound, he stepped out. The door closed soundlessly.

Joey raced to the shed. He noticed that it was really a shabby-looking building. Grandpa had built it with old lumber he had collected. He planned to paint it. But his sickness had made that impossible.

Click. The padlock opened as Joey turned the key. He opened the latch, turned the doorknob on the old door, and stepped into the shed. He pulled the door shut behind him.

*Mom will never look for me here,* Joey thought. He walked through the darkness of the shed. The only light to be seen came in through the crack at the bottom of the door. Joey had helped grandpa build the shed, but he had forgotten that they had not cut the holes where the windows were to be.

Joey felt his way slowly around the shed. He decided it was about the same size as his bedroom.

He knelt down by the door. He held his arm by the crack at the bottom of the door so he could see his watch. *It's five after three,* he said to himself. *Mom should be coming home about now.*

Silently Joey sat down on the cold cement floor. He could not hear a sound from outside except for the wind which was blowing slightly. Joey tried to figure out what his mom and Jennifer would do when they couldn't find him. *They will probably look all over the house,* he decided. *Then they will call Mike's place, and maybe a few of my other friends. They will never look here.*

He sat in complete silence. His mind kept working though. *Uncle Jeff and Aunt Chris are supposed to get here between five and six. When mom can't find me, she and Jenn will go to the nursing home without me so they can be back home by the time Jeff and Chris get here.*

All at once Joey realized that the wind was beginning to blow harder. It almost whistled as it blew past the shed. The dampness of his coat made the dark cold of the shed seem even colder. He decided, *I'll stay here until about 3:30.*

*What can I tell mom when she gets home from the nursing home?* he asked himself. *I could tell her that I decided to run downtown to try to buy another gift of some kind. But then I would have told Jenn where I was going.* He concluded, *Maybe I will just have to tell her the truth. She knows that I can't stand that nursing home. Maybe she won't be too mad. She understands how I hate to see grandpa so sick and weak.*

His thoughts were interrupted by the howl of the wind. It sounded like a real storm outside. When he returned to the crack to check the time again, he discovered that snow was blowing under the door.

*Mom and Jenn have surely given up on finding me by now,* he said to himself. *But I better wait five or ten minutes more just to be sure.*

The cold was starting to bother him. He discovered that he did not have his mittens in his coat pockets. They were in the house getting dried out from the morning snowball fight. He walked around slowly. He pushed his chilly hands deep into his coat pockets. He stopped. Pressing an ear against the rough wood of the wall closest to the house, he listened. He heard only the constant wind.

*It's got to be safe to leave now,* he decided. He grabbed the doorknob and turned it. It went *snap!*

"Oh, no," Joey cried. The doorknob from that old door Grandpa Lane had put on the shed broke right off. Joey tried to put it back on the door, but everything had broken off completely.

Dropping the useless knob to the floor, he tried to push the door open. It wouldn't budge. He tried kicking the door. That only hurt his feet.

*If I only had something to smash the door open,* he thought. But there was nothing in the shed except for that useless old doorknob.

Joey was becoming afraid. He realized that he was trapped. "Help!" he shouted. "Help! Help!" He pounded and kicked furiously at the door as he shouted. He was overflowing with panic. But he knew that the noise of the blizzard kept him from being heard very far from the shed.

"What am I going to do?" he moaned. He backed away from the door and slumped back

to the floor. Tears of fear forged their way out. Joey pulled his knees up toward his chest as he sat on the cold floor. He put his arms on his knees and his head on his arms. *What can I do now?* he wondered. *I could freeze to death before anyone finds me out here.*

Joey cried for a long time. When he stopped crying, he sat in silence and listened to the angry, taunting sound of the wind. He felt totally helpless. He tried to think of a way to get out, but his mind was all mixed up and he could not think of a thing.

The dampness of Joey's jacket was making him extra miserable. He went back to the crack. *I've been here for over an hour,* he thought. It was ten after four. He felt his knees getting wet and cold as he knelt in the thin layer of snow that had drifted in under the door.

Standing up again, Joey put his mouth near the door and shouted as loud as he could. "Help! Help!" He shouted many times. He listened. The only answer he got was the moaning of the wind as it swirled around the shed.

Joey sniffed a couple of times. His body was starting to ache from the cold. He was getting mad at himself. "Why didn't I grab some mittens?" he said angrily. Whenever he took his hands out of his pockets his fingers felt almost numb. He pulled the hood on his coat tighter, but his fingers felt so stiff he could hardly handle the strings from the hood.

*Maybe some exercises would warm me up*, he thought. He did some jumping-jacks. He ran in place. He swung his arms around and around. It helped. He felt a little better.

*I'll bet mom and Jenn are home now*, Joey said to himself. *It must be 4:30.* His thoughts flowed on as he sat down again. *I wonder what they will do when they still don't find me. They have to look here sometime.*

Joey tried to think of something to do to forget about the cold. He decided to count to one hundred slowly. He would let about five seconds pass between each number. *They'll find me before I reach a hundred*, he thought confidently.

He reached 100. Still no one came. He thought of many things to kill time. He listened for sounds outside. All he ever heard was the wind. He went to the crack a couple of more times to check the time. He did some more exercises, but he still felt cold through and through. His toes hurt and were numb at the same time. He blew on his hands, but they still felt cold. He could not stop shivering. He had never felt this cold before. He could not get warm at all anymore.

Suddenly Joey became even more afraid. "No," he cried aloud, "it's dark out." He went to check the time at the crack when he realized that there was no more light coming in. He had not thought about night coming. *I've got to get out now,* he thought. He screamed and screamed for help. The wind was not blowing as hard. But no one came to his rescue.

Again that feeling of panic engulfed him. He tried to push the door open again. It refused to move at all. He backed away from the door. He ran at the door and rammed it with his shoulder. One, two, three times. The door didn't move. He tried again. This time he suddenly felt a sharp pain in his shoulder. In the darkness he had missed the door and hit the frame around it.

"This is hopeless," he cried. Joey turned his back to the door and tried to kick it open again. He kicked like a horse kicking at a stable door. Still nothing happened! Finally, Joey tried to kick so hard that he slipped on the wet snow that had blown under the door. He hit the floor with a thud. His forehead hit the cement. "Ow," he cried.

Hopelessly Joey struggled to his feet again. He touched his forehead. There didn't seem to be any blood. But even with his numbed fingers he could feel a big, aching lump. He moved away from the door. Slumping against a wall, he slid back down to the floor.

*What am I doing here?* he asked himself. *Why didn't I go with mom and Jenn to see grandpa?*

*That would have been better than this.* One thought after another rambled across his tired brain. *I wonder what time it is. Will they ever find me? What a terrible place to have to spend Christmas. Am I going to die here?*

He was freezing cold. His head and shoulder both hurt so much. Joey had no idea what time it was. He was so weary and tired. Like a little lost child, he cried and cried.

Through his tears, he prayed, "O God, help me."

## 4

## A LESSON

"Maybe I better call the police." Karen Andrews looked around at the people in her kitchen. A few neighbors were sitting around the kitchen table. Others were standing. No one said a word, but all of their faces reflected worry. "Joey has been gone for almost four hours," she said. "What do you think, Jeff?"

"I don't know, Sis," answered Jeff Lane. Uncle Jeff was her only brother. Jeff and his wife Chris had just arrived from their home about 200 miles away to spend Christmas with Grandpa Lane and with the Andrews family. The snowstorm had caused them to arrive later than they had planned.

"Are you sure you have looked everywhere for him?" Jeff inquired.

"I have called everyone I can think of," said Mrs. Andrews. "We have been driving all around

Forestburg. We've looked at all of the places where Joey and his friends play. We just can't find him."

Jack Tyler, Mike's dad, spoke up. "We have been looking all over for him too, Jeff." Mr. Tyler was leaning against the refrigerator. He went on, "We have talked to Mike and all of Joey's other friends. No one has any idea where he is."

Jeff leaned back in his chair. He scratched his head and then pushed back his long reddish-brown hair. He looked at his niece and said, "Jenn, are you sure Joey didn't say something about where he was going?"

"No, Uncle Jeff," she said. "I was wrapping Christmas presents in the family room. We were waiting for mom to get home from work. Joey was in the kitchen. All at once he was gone. I didn't even hear him leave."

Karen Andrews interrupted her daughter to explain. "I had insisted that Joey had to go with us to the nursing home today. For some reason he hates that place." Sadness covered her face as she spoke. "When I came home and Jenn told me he was gone, we looked all around the house. I called a few of his friends. No one had seen him or talked to him. Then, when I saw that his coat was gone, I decided that he had taken off for a while so he would not have to go with us." She was near tears as she finished telling of what had happened. "But that was at three o'clock. It is almost seven now. Something must have happened to him."

"Now try not to worry, Karen," said Mike's mother, Ann Tyler. "He will probably show up soon."

Cora Lucas, an elderly widow who lived just down the street, added, "Sure, he will. You know how boys forget about the time."

"I hope you are right," said Joey's mother. "But it is Christmas Eve. Something must have happened to him or he would have been home by now."

She got up from her chair. "I think I have to call the police. Maybe they can help find Joey." She stopped before she got to the phone and looked around at the neighbors gathered in her kitchen. "Why don't you all go home?" she suggested. "You have been so helpful. I have been so worried about Joey that I haven't even given you anything to eat. You have all missed dinner. Your families will be starved." She added, "It is Christmas Eve. You really should be with your families now."

For a moment no one answered. No one knew what to do or say. Then Jack Tyler spoke up. "We want to stay a little longer. You go ahead and call the police, but we want to help you try to think of where Joey can be."

"But it isn't necessary for all of you to stay," insisted Mrs. Andrews. "Jeff and Chris are here, and I am going to call. . . ."

"We are staying a little longer," interrupted Mr. Tyler. "We are worried about Joey, too."

"Okay," Joey's mom agreed. "Let me put some coffee on though." As she turned on one of the burners on the stove she added, "Jenn, get a plate for some cookies."

Jennifer got a plate and covered it with chocolate-chip cookies. She was getting cups out of the cupboard when one slipped out of her hand. Crash! It smashed into many pieces on the floor.

"Oh, Jenn." Her mother sounded angry. "Watch what you are doing! Now get a broom and clean that up."

"I'll help, Jenn," offered Uncle Jeff. He could see that she was almost ready to cry.

"No," Jennifer murmured, "I'll take care of it."

She went to the closet in the back hall to get a broom and a dustpan. She was turning to go back to the kitchen when she saw the empty nail in the closet.

"Mom," she called quickly, "the key for grandpa's shed is gone. Have you seen it?"

Jack Tyler asked, "Did anyone look in the shed?"

"We didn't," said Mrs. Andrews. "I didn't even think about looking out there. Maybe Joey went there. But he wouldn't stay there this long unless something is wrong."

She hardly finished what she was saying when Uncle Jeff and Jack Tyler were out the back door with a flashlight in hand. They didn't even take time to put their coats and boots on.

Joey jumped. He had fallen asleep, and the sudden sound of someone at the door startled him. The door was jerked open. A flashlight was shining on him.

"Joey." He could tell it was Uncle Jeff's voice.

He tried to jump up, but he was so stiff and numb that he could hardly move. "Uncle Jeff, am I glad to see you," shouted Joey.

"Are you all right?" asked Mr. Tyler.

"I think so," answered Joey. "I'm freezing though, especially my toes and my fingers." Joey was standing now. "I feel so stiff I can hardly move."

Uncle Jeff said, "We will get you warmed up right away." Without saying another word, Jeff picked up Joey and put him over his shoulder as a fireman would do. In less than a minute Jeff had carried Joey back through the snow drifts and into the house.

When Karen Andrews saw her brother carry Joey into the house she cried, "Oh, Joey, Joey."

Jennifer asked, "Are you okay? What happened to you?"

Joey was so glad to be in the house that he laughed and cried all at once. His mother hugged and kissed him. She was crying too. "Oh, I am so thankful you are all right," she said. "Thank God you are here."

The neighbors stayed at the Andrews house long enough to find out what had happened. They all told Joey and his mother how happy they were that he was safe. With a "Merry Christmas" the neighbors all went to their homes and families.

Aunt Chris was a nurse. Because Joey had been exposed to the cold for so long, she put cold, damp cloths on his cheeks, nose, and ears. She also had Joey soak his feet and hands in cold water. By the time the Christmas Eve dinner was ready, Joey felt much better. The stinging and numbness caused by the cold was gone. Even his sore shoulder and the bump on his forehead didn't hurt so much anymore.

It was almost midnight when Joey finally tumbled into bed. They had opened their presents. It had been a night of laughing and talking and just being happy for their family.

As his mother tucked him into bed, she gave him another big hug and a kiss. "I am so thankful you are all right," she said. "I was so worried about you." As she turned out his light she added, "It has been such a good Christmas Eve. Now say your prayers and try to go right to sleep. We are all going to church tomorrow morning for the Christmas Day service."

Joey was so tired that he didn't even think much about the new hockey game, the basketball, and other presents he had received. His prayer was short. "God, thank you for helping me even when I did such a foolish thing as to try to run away and hide."

His shoulder and head still hurt some, but he was sound asleep in less than a minute.

The next morning, the Christmas Day service was coming to an end. They finished singing "Joy to the World." Joey put the hymnal back in the hymnal rack in the church pew. Everyone seemed to be smiling and saying "Merry Christmas" to everyone else as they left the church.

"Merry Christmas, Joey," said Pastor Don as he shook Joey's hand at the door.

Joey replied, "Merry Christmas."

"Can you wait just a couple of minutes, Joey?" asked the pastor. "I would like to talk to you for a little while."

"All right," said Joey, as he walked over near where the guestbook was. He waited until Pastor Don finished shaking hands with everyone.

Pastor Don had his hymnal under his arm as he came to the place where Joey was standing. He said, "I hear you had a real adventure yesterday."

"I guess so," answered Joey quietly. He was

not anxious to talk about what had happened. He was not proud of what he had done.

"I understand you were out in your grandfather's shed all through the storm. That is quite a bruise you got on your forehead," commented Pastor Don. "Do you feel all right today?"

Joey smiled as he answered, "I feel real good now. I am just glad that they found me when they did."

"That is kind of what I want to talk to you about, Joey," said the pastor. "Come with me to my office. We can talk while I change. I told your mother that I will give you a ride home."

When they entered Pastor Don's office, Joey sat down in one of the chairs near the desk. "Joey," the pastor began to speak again, "we are all very thankful that you are okay. But I thought this would be a good time to talk about something else. Did you know that a lot of people were trying to help find you yesterday?"

"Yes," said Joey. He liked Pastor Don a lot. But he could not figure out what he was driving at.

"I want you to know that many people were out driving around looking for you during that snowstorm yesterday. That was dangerous," added Pastor Don, "because people could hardly see to drive. Some people were making phone calls. Even though it was Christmas Eve, the Tylers, Mrs. Lucas, and others forgot all about their own families and stayed with your mother until you were found."

Joey didn't know what to say. He looked at all of the books that lined the shelves of the pastor's office as he listened.

"What I am saying, Joey, is this. These people all would have preferred to be at home yesterday afternoon and last night. They would have rather been eating and opening gifts with their families. But because they care about you and your mother and Jennifer, they did what they did instead. That is part of being a Christian." He kept talking as he pulled his coat on. "We are all supposed to be like your neighbors were last night. We may prefer to be doing something else, but we do what is right . . . what is best. Do you see what I am saying?" the pastor asked.

"Yes," said Joey quietly. His voice squeaked as he said it. "We do what is right instead of what we want to do."

"Exactly," smiled Pastor Don. "Now I want you to think about Grandpa Lane for a minute. I visit him quite often." The pastor sat down behind the desk. "He really misses you, you know. He has asked me why you never come to see him. I said I don't know. Then I talked to your mother about it. She explained that you simply don't want to go to the nursing home. Right?"

"Right," said Joey. He stared at the floor. "I

don't like the people there, and I don't like to see grandpa so weak and sick."

"I can understand that," said Pastor Don. "But remember, sometimes we should do what we really don't want to do. Think again about those people who were out looking for you yesterday. They did it because they care about you."

Joey was beginning to understand what the pastor was driving at. "Now," said Pastor Don, "if you care about your grandfather, and I know you do, maybe you better go and visit him even if you would rather stay home or play with your friends." Pastor Don paused to let Joey think about what he had just said. Then he continued, "I think Christmas Day would be a perfect time to go to see him. You know he might not be here next Christmas."

"Maybe you're right," said Joey. Joey knew he was right, but he still did not want to go.

"Listen, Joey," said Pastor Don, "I don't want to preach to you, and I don't want to force you to do something you don't want to do. But I do want you to think about what others did for you and about what you can do for your grandfather. Okay?"

"Okay," said Joey. "I'll think about it."

"Good," said the pastor. "Now I better get you home."

Pastor Don's car was just turning on to Oak

Street a block from Joey's home when Joey announced, "I am going to see Grandpa Lane today."

"Are you sure?" asked the pastor.

"Yup," answered Joey. "I have made up my mind."

The pastor smiled and said, "That's good news. I am sure that you will make your grandfather's Christmas a lot happier."

"Thanks for the ride," said Joey, "and for the lesson."

The car stopped. "Thank you for taking time to talk to me," replied Pastor Don. "I'll see you, Joey. Have a happy Christmas."

"Bye," said Joey.

As he walked toward the house, Joey was making plans. "I'm going. It is going to be awful going to that place, but I have to go to see grandpa. No matter what, I'll go right after dinner."

## 5

## CHRISTMAS REUNION

"Are you sure you don't want me to go with you to see grandpa?" asked Uncle Jeff. He and Joey were walking toward the front door of the Forest View Nursing Home.

"No," said Joey, "I want to see grandpa alone."

"All right," said Uncle Jeff. "But I will ask the lady at the information desk if you can call us when you are through in grandpa's room. Then I will come and get you."

Joey felt a weakness in his knees as they crossed the lobby. He did not really want to go to see grandpa alone, but he knew he had to apologize to grandpa for not coming for so long. He didn't want anyone else to hear that.

"Good, she's not there," Joey thought as he looked down the long hall toward grandpa's room. He was worried about that woman who had grabbed his jacket sleeve.

He heard Uncle Jeff's voice. "It's all set, Joey. When you are through visiting with grandpa, you stop at the desk. They will call us."

"Thanks," said Joey.

"Have fun," said Uncle Jeff. "And tell grandpa that the rest of us will be here to see him later this afternoon."

"I'll tell him," said Joey.

A nervous Joey started down what appeared to be an endless hallway toward Room 127. "I would rather go anywhere else if I could," thought Joey. He slowly made his way down the hall as though he were in fear of being ambushed. He let out a sigh of relief when he came to grandpa's room without seeing that woman who had scared him so.

Grandpa Lane appeared to be sleeping in a wheelchair as Joey stepped into his room. "Hello, grandpa," said Joey cheerfully. "Merry Christmas."

Grandpa's head jerked up. A look of surprise crossed his face. "Joey," he said happily, "am I glad to see you!" He quickly added, "Why, come in, pal. We had such a big Christmas dinner. I was just dozing off a little."

Joey said, "I am glad to see you, too."

Grandpa held out his hand, and Joey shook it. His hand felt weak and thin. Once his hands had been so big and strong. He looked even weaker and more tired than the first time Joey visited him at the nursing home.

"How do you like my Christmas presents?" asked grandpa as he motioned to the new multi-colored robe and the red slippers he was wearing.

"They really look nice," answered Joey. He had bought the slippers for grandpa. Jenn had picked out the colorful robe. Joey's mother told him that she had wrapped the slippers and taken them to the nursing home for him while he was hiding in the shed.

Grandpa's eyes twinkled as he continued on. "But do you know what the best Christmas present of all is?" He didn't wait for Joey to answer. "Seeing you is the best present of all."

Joey still felt nervous and uncomfortable. He was ashamed that it had been such a long time since he had seen his grandfather. "Grandpa," Joey started bashfully, "I'm very sorry that I haven't been here for such a long time."

"Oh, that's all right. You had other things to do," said grandpa.

"No," said Joey apologetically, "I know now that I should have come back sooner. But—but, I don't like this place. I'm sorry, but I just don't like it here. I promise, though, that I will come more often from now on."

"Okay," said grandpa, with that familiar understanding smile on his face. "Now let's forget about that. You just pull up a chair and sit down. Let's talk and enjoy ourselves like we used to do."

Joey pulled a chair closer to grandpa's wheelchair and sat down. "How are you feeling today?" Joey asked.

Grandpa replied, "I really feel quite well, but am so weak. That is why I spend so much time in this Cadillac." Grandpa slapped the arm rests on his wheelchair. "I need the Cadillac because I just can't walk anymore." Grandpa chuckled as he joked about his wheelchair.

Joey was glad to hear that old familiar chuckle, even if it did sound weaker now.

"Say, pal, when your uncle Jeff came here after church this morning, he hold me about what happened to you in the old shed yesterday," said grandpa. "What happened anyway?"

Joey told the whole story about the shed.

"You have got yourself quite a bruise on your head," observed grandpa. "It's a real honey. I'll have to fix that door knob when I get back home."

Joey quickly looked down. He knew grandpa would never be back home again. When he looked up, he saw such a sad expression on grandpa's face. Grandpa too realized what he had said, and that he would not be coming home again.

Grandpa Lane quickly changed the subject and called out, "Say, Eldon, are you awake?"

"I sure am," came a reply from the other side

of the curtain that ran through the center of the room.

"Pull the curtain, will you?" said Grandpa. "I want you to meet someone."

In no time at all the curtain was pulled back and Joey saw an old, dignified looking man. Like grandpa, he had neatly combed gray hair. Unlike grandpa, he was dressed in regular clothes.

"Joey, this is Eldon Slater. Eldon's from over at Kellerton." Grandpa motioned toward Joey and said, "Eldon, this is my grandson, Joey Andrews. He's my best pal."

"I'm pleased to meet you Joey," said Mr. Slater in a strong, healthy voice. He got up from his bed, where he had been sitting. Putting down the book he was reading, he walked over to where Joey was sitting and shook hands. "Any friend of your grandfather's is a friend of mine," he said with a smile.

"I'm glad to meet you, too," said Joey. Joey liked Mr. Slater immediately.

Mr. Slater said, "I hope to see more of you, Joey. I will let you two visit now. I am hoping my two sons and their families will be coming to visit me today. They haven't come to visit me in the five weeks I have been here." Then he added hopefully, "But they only live about forty miles from here at Kellerton. I think they will be here today because it's Christmas. I am going down to the lobby to wait for them."

"I will see you later," said Joey, as Mr. Slater left the room.

Joey and Grandpa Lane talked for a long time. They both laughed as they remembered funny things that had happened. Grandpa looked so good and so happy as they reminisced that at times Joey forgot about his illness.

Grandpa Lane was just telling about a snowstorm that they had one Christmas Eve when he was young when a nurse looked in the door. "Come in," called grandpa quickly. "I want you to meet my grandson."

"I am just checking to see if everything is all right," said the nurse.

Joey stood up as grandpa started to introduce him. "Joey, meet one of my new girlfriends, Sarah Kinney." The young nurse blushed. Grandpa added, "This is my grandson, Joey Andrews."

Miss Kinney stayed in the room for a couple of minutes. Grandpa enjoyed teasing her, and she didn't seem to mind it at all. It made Joey feel good to see that his grandpa could still laugh and joke even when he was so sick.

Joey had been in Room 127 for over an hour when he realized that Grandpa Lane was starting to look very tired. Joey suggested, "I think I better leave, grandpa. Uncle Jeff and Aunt Chris and mom and Jenn are going to come to see you later this afternoon. You probably should sleep a little before they come."

"I guess I could use some rest," admitted grandpa. "Talking to you today has been the most fun I have had for a long time. It has been just like old times."

Joey spoke honestly, "I am really glad I came to see you today, grandpa."

"Thanks, pal," said grandpa, as Joey got up to leave. "Have a merry Christmas. You have really made mine very happy and complete."

Joey squeezed grandpa's right hand extra hard as he shook it. He said, "Merry Christmas, grandpa. I'll be back soon."

There were tears in grandpa's eyes as Joey left the room. But they were tears of happiness, joy, and contentment.

Joey felt a warm glow inside as he walked out of grandpa's room. *Sure,* he thought, *Grandpa is sick and weak. But he looked so happy.* He wondered, *Why did I stay away so long?* as he walked toward the lobby.

All at once Joey looked up. There she was! That woman who had grabbed him the first time he visited grandpa stood right in the middle of the hall. He had forgotten all about her. She was less than ten feet ahead of Joey.

He felt a surge of fear and panic. She stood

and stared at him. He thought, *She looks even worse than before. Her hair looks terrible. Her sweater is even buttoned wrong.*

The woman started to walk slowly toward him. She was coming closer and closer! Joey had to get away from her.

He turned to run. He didn't know where he would run to, but he had to get away. Boom! He just started to run when he ran smack into a white nurse's uniform. It was Miss Kinney as she was coming out of a room. He almost knocked her over, and she grabbed him to keep her balance.

"I'm sorry," Joey blurted it out fast.

"That's all right. I'm not hurt," said the young nurse. "You were surely running like a fullback. Is something wrong?"

Joey felt foolish.

"Are you okay?" asked Miss Kinney.

Joey nodded. He smiled, trying to convince her that everything was all right, even though he had bumped that sore shoulder.

"Is something wrong?" asked the nurse.

"No," said Joey quickly. He knew something was wrong. But he didn't dare tell her that he was terrified by an old woman.

"Are you sure nothing is wrong?" she asked. The nurse could tell that Joey was very excited. He was breathing hard.

Just then that old woman came to where Joey and Miss Kinney were standing. She grabbed Joey's sleeve again. Miss Kinney noticed the fear in Joey's eyes as he looked at the old woman. He tried to pull his arm free from her grip without running away.

"Hazel, this isn't your boy." Miss Kinney spoke gently to the woman as she took her hand and lifted it from Joey's sleeve. The nurse said, "You go back to your room now, Hazel. I will come and visit you in a little while."

Obediently, almost like a robot, the woman turned and shuffled back toward her room. Joey noticed that she just slid her feet along the floor as she walked.

Joey was relieved!

"Were you trying to get away from her, Joey?" asked the nurse. "Is that what you were afraid of when you ran into me?"

Joey felt so cowardly. "Yes," he said meekly.

Miss Kinney said, "Don't feel bad about that. I'm afraid Hazel scares quite a few people until they get to know her. She is really so gentle. She would never hurt anybody." The nurse continued, "You see, Hazel's only boy died when he was about eleven or twelve years old. It really upset her. That was many, many years ago. Now that she is old, she has gotten confused. Her mind is mixed up and she keeps looking for her boy. She won't accept the fact that he died. And unfortunately," the nurse sighed, "she doesn't care how she looks, and she won't let us help her fix her hair and dress her."

Joey listened with interest as Miss Kinney kept talking. "When she grabbed your arm, she wanted to talk to you. She thinks that every boy who comes by her room might be her son. If she ever takes you by the arm again, tell her your name, and tell her that you are not her son. She will let you go. Hazel hardly talks at all anymore, but she will understand."

Looking toward the lobby, Joey could see the old woman standing in the doorway to her room. He still was not sure he wanted to go past her. Miss Kinney could see that.

"Come on, Joey," she said, "I will introduce you to Hazel. Maybe she will remember you from now on and won't bother you."

"Okay," Joey murmured.

Joey was still a little scared as they walked to where the old woman was standing. They walked slowly as Miss Kinney was refastening her nurse's cap, which Joey had almost knocked from her head in the collision.

"Hazel, I want you to meet someone," said the young nurse. "This is Joey. His grandpa lives here." The old woman smiled. Joey had not seen her smile before. It was actually a warm, friendly smile. "Joey, this is Mrs. Duncan. Hazel Duncan."

"Hul-lo," said Mrs. Duncan slowly. She didn't say it very clearly, but she kept smiling. She wanted to shake hands.

Joey smiled back nervously and said, "Hi." He was not so sure he wanted to shake hands with her. But then he reached out and took her warm, soft hand. "I—I—I'm glad to meet you, Mrs. Duncan," said Joey. Then he blurted out, "Merry Christmas."

Mrs. Duncan didn't say anything. She nodded though, and her smile got a little bigger.

Miss Kinney spoke up. "Joey has to go home now, Hazel."

"Goodbye," said Joey.

Mrs. Duncan kept smiling.

Miss Kinney walked with Joey toward the lobby and the information desk. Her hands were in the pockets of her white uniform as she spoke. "Joey, most of the people here are able to talk and visit like your grandfather. They just need some special care, like Grandpa Lane. Some don't see well. Some are hard of hearing. Some can't walk anymore. Others just need a place to live. A few, like Hazel, are rather mixed up." She smiled as she added. "They are all people though. They still need love and kindness just like you and I do. And remember, they don't want to hurt anyone."

70

"I'll remember that," said Joey.

"Should I call your uncle now?" asked the woman at the information desk.

"Yes," said Joey.

"I better get back to work now," said Miss Kinney. "It has been nice talking to you, Joey. I'll see you again."

"Thank you," said Joey. He meant it because he appreciated her kindness and understanding. "I'll be back soon."

"Good," said the nurse, as she started down the hall again.

Joey was walking toward the door when he saw Mr. Slater sitting in a soft chair in the lobby.

"Are you still waiting for your sons?" Joey asked.

Mr. Slater looked at Joey and nodded slowly. "I am. But I guess they aren't coming again today." The old gentleman looked out the big windows toward the driveway and parking area. There was sadness in his eyes and in his voice.

Joey knew why he was sad. It was because someone didn't care enough to come to visit. Joey knew all about those who stay away.

Uncle Jeff's car was coming down the driveway toward the nursing home. "Merry Christmas," said Joey.

"Thank you," said Mr. Slater. As Joey was pushing the front door open, Mr. Slater added,

"Joey, be sure to come and see your grandpa again soon. He talks about you so much."

"I will," said Joey as he stepped outside.

"I still don't like that place very much," Joey muttered to himself as he neared Uncle Jeff's car. "I hate the thought of seeing grandpa when he gets real sick and dies."

Joey jumped into the car. "Boy, Uncle Jeff, it sure was fun to see grandpa again."

## 6

## A SPECIAL VISIT

"Man, what a day for a ballgame," said Joey as he and Mike shot through the doorway of the Washington Elementary School and into the April sunlight.

"Yeah," said Mike. "I'm not even going to put my jacket on."

It was spring. Snow was nowhere to be seen. The grass was turning green. A few leaves were making their appearance on the trees in front of the school.

Joey waved frantically at one of the school buses as it pulled away from the curb. "Tim, Tim, Tim." He called until a boy sitting by one of the bus windows turned his head quickly. "Be sure to bring your glove tomorrow," shouted Joey.

The quick nodding of Tim's head indicated that he had heard Joey's reminder.

Baseball was the topic of discussion as the two

boys walked the six blocks toward their homes on Oak Street. Mike said, "A bunch of guys from our room are meeting at Lincoln Park at four for a game."

"Great," said Joey happily. "I'm supposed to call some of the guys from our room if we can get a game together. I'll call them as soon as I get home."

"I can't believe how warm it is," said Mike, as he swung his jacket over his shoulder.

Joey gripped the math book he was carrying in both hands. Pretending it was a baseball bat, he took a couple of swings with it. "I can hardly wait to start hitting that ball," he said.

When Joey reached his house he suggested, "Let's ride our bikes over to the park."

Mike agreed.

"It will take me a little while to call some of the guys," advised Joey. "But I'll be ready to go by four. Okay?"

"Good," said Mike, as he crossed the street to his house.

Joey was devouring three brownies and a glass of milk when the phone rang. It was his mother calling from work.

"Is Jenn home yet, Honey?" she asked.

Joey hated it when she called him Honey. That was no name for a boy who would soon be in junior high. "I don't think she is home yet," he replied. "I haven't seen her."

"Listen," her voice sounded very serious. "I got a call from the nursing home this morning. Grandpa Lane is feeling worse. They don't know if he will live much longer." Joey listened carefully as she continued. "I went to see him at noon. He was real bad. I think you and Jenn should walk over to the nursing home to visit him right away. Do it as soon as Jenn gets home from school."

"I can't go now," said Joey. "Maybe we can go tonight, right after we eat. We've got a big ballgame planned at four. Mike and I . . ."

"I'm sorry but you have got to go now," his mother interrupted. "We are invited to the Tylers' for dinner tonight. After we eat, they are going to show us the pictures from the trip they took after Christmas." She added, "There won't be time then."

Joey protested. "Do I have to go today? I really don't want to go now."

"Now, Joey." Mrs. Andrews voice had that very definite sound to it. "You have been visiting grandpa two or three times a week since Christmas. You have been enjoying it, and you know how he waits for you to come. I insist that you go today. It might be one of the last times grandpa will be able to talk to you."

"Okay," Joey mumbled. Then he spoke almost

in anger. "This is the first decent day we have had for baseball. I don't see why I have to go to that dumb nursing home."

"I don't want any more of that kind of talk from you, young man." His mother's voice was sharp.

Joey said, "I'm sorry." He knew that Grandpa Lane was more important than a ballgame. "I think Jenn just came in. We'll walk over there right away."

"That's better," said Mrs. Andrews. "I just hope grandpa will still be able to talk to you. He was so weak and sleepy at noon." She added, "I should be home at about 5:30."

"Okay, mom," said Joey. "Goodbye."

"Goodbye," she replied. "And Joey, thanks for doing this."

Joey explained the call to Jennifer. He still wasn't very happy, but they left on their journey to the nursing home.

"Well I declare, it's Charlie and Elizabeth." The friendly voice and smile of Mr. Slater greeted Jennifer and Joey as they entered Room 127 at Forest View Nursing Home. "Charlie and Elizabeth" were the special names that he had given to Joey and Jennifer. He enjoyed teasing them.

"Hi, Mr. Slater," answered Joey. "How is grandpa today?"

Mr. Slater shook his head from side to side, in-

dicating that grandpa was not feeling well at all. "He hasn't been out of bed for over a week," said Mr. Slater.

Joey was startled when he looked at Grandpa Lane. He was so terribly thin. He hardly moved. *He doesn't look at all like he once did*, thought Joey sadly.

Grandpa appeared to be sleeping as they entered the room. He opened his eyes as they came near his bed. He gave them a smile. It too looked so weak.

"Hi," whispered grandpa.

Jennifer and Joey both said, "Hi, grandpa."

"How are you today?" asked Joey.

Grandpa said, "I'm not very good, pal."

"You look tired." Jennifer spoke with real concern.

"I am tired, Jenny. And I am so weak." Grandpa's answer was just a whisper. "I can't eat anything anymore. I guess I have about run out of gas."

"What do you mean?" asked Joey.

Grandpa said nothing for awhile. He thought. Then he spoke. "Well," he whispered, "I am like an old engine that won't run much longer. I am all worn out. I think I am about through on this earth."

Joey didn't like that kind of talk. "Oh grandpa," he broke in, "We don't want to talk about that."

"Just a minute, Joey." Grandpa had something he wanted to tell them. "We are going to talk about it. I remember when you all came to visit me the first day I was here. You asked me about death. I didn't want to talk about it then. I got angry." He was speaking slowly, choosing each word with care, as though he didn't have many words left. "Death upset me then. I even got mad at God for letting me get sick. But now I want to talk about it."

Jennifer and Joey said nothing. They both moved closer to the bed to hear grandpa's weak, sometimes trembling, voice.

Grandpa continued, "I know now that my life is nearly over."

"Now, grandpa . . ." Joey was going to change the subject.

"No, let me finish." Grandpa was almost pleading. "I am not afraid to die now. I have been doing a lot of thinking about the promises of God and about my faith." His voice was filled with confidence, in spite of his weakness. "God has given me a feeling of calm and a certainty that I will be with him when I die."

He paused. He seemed to be having trouble getting his breath. Then he went on. "I don't know what it will be like when I die, but I do know that Jesus will take care of me. And, I know that somehow I will be with him because he loves me and because I trust him. He will raise me and I will be with him."

"That's good," said Jennifer gently.

Joey didn't know what to say.

Grandpa managed another weak smile. He was tired. He had no strength left. Not a muscle moved as he lay there. But he wanted to keep talking. "There is something else I want to tell you two while I can. While I have been lying here, I have been thinking about life. I want you to know that you should use your life, each one of you." He kept whispering. "I have been thinking about my life. I have used my life in many ways. I tried to be the kind of man God wants me to be. I tried to help those who needed me . . . like you two and your mother."

He still lay motionless. Grandpa looked straight at both of them and spoke with all of the strength he could muster. "Now I want you to use your lives too. Your mom is going to need a lot of help. You will find other people to love and help too. That is what life is for."

A smile crossed that thin face. "Okay, pals?"

"Okay, grandpa," answered Joey.

"Okay," added Jennifer.

No one spoke for a moment. Joey was thinking. No one had ever talked to him about life and death like that before.

Jennifer took one of grandpa's hands. "I love you, grandpa," she said.

"Me too," added Joey. He felt sad, like he was ready to cry.

Grandpa Lane smiled again. Then he closed his eyes and seemed to doze off for a nap.

Jennifer and Joey quietly walked over to where Mr. Slater was sitting.

"What are you reading today?" asked Joey.

"Aw, it's another murder mystery," said Mr. Slater. "I think I have got it figured out already though."

Mr. Slater put down the book. In his many visits to Grandpa Lane, Joey had discovered that Mr. Slater had been a school teacher for many years. He still loved books. He was always sending Miss Kinney or someone else from the nursing home to the library to get books for him. Joey was amazed that Mr. Slater never wore glasses. He was well over eighty years old, and he read constantly.

"I suppose you are ready for spring training with weather like this," said Mr. Slater.

"I sure am," said Joey. "We were going to have a game this afternoon. Then we heard that grandpa wasn't very good."

"I'm glad the two of you came," said Mr. Slater. "Your grandfather always seems to feel so much better after you come to visit him."

Mr. Slater got up from his chair and walked to the night-stand near his bed. He opened the top drawer. "I just happen to have a little something for the two of you," he said. Pulling out a couple of bags of candy, he tossed them to Jennifer and Joey.

Both Jennifer and Joey said, "Thank you."

Joey felt sorry for Mr. Slater. He enjoyed visiting people so much. He was so intelligent. His children and grandchildren hardly ever came to visit him. Maybe that was why he was always so anxious to visit with Jennifer and Joey. He always had something to give them.

"By the way, Charlie," said Mr. Slater as he sat down again, "what is red and black and red and black and red and black?"

Joey thought. "I don't know," he said.

"How about you, Elizabeth?"

"Me neither," responded Jennifer.

"It's a checkerboard," chuckled Mr. Slater. He always seemed to have funny, sometimes silly, riddles. His eyes sparkled whenever he was able to stump them.

There was a sound from Grandpa Lane's bed. Grandpa's eyes were open again. He was looking at them.

Returning to Grandpa's bed, Jennifer said, "We better go now. It takes us quite a while to walk home."

In silence, Joey stood beside Jennifer.

"Thanks for coming," grandpa whispered. "Remember what I told you."

Jennifer said, "We will. Goodbye, grandpa."

"Goodbye, Jenny," he said. "Goodbye, pal."

Joey and Grandpa Lane exchanged loving smiles. Joey felt so sad. "Goodbye, grandpa," he said.

When they were outside of Room 127, Jennifer and Joey looked back toward grandpa. He managed another weak smile, and he raised one hand barely enough so he could wave at them. They waved back.

As they walked down the hall they said nothing to each other. They did stop long enough to say hello to Mrs. Simon, their mother's old typing teacher.

As usual Mrs. Duncan was standing by her door. "Hello, Mrs. Duncan," said Joey. He wasn't afraid of her anymore.

She gave her usual, "Hul-lo." With it came a big, happy smile.

Jennifer and Joey were both very quiet as they walked toward home.

Jennifer broke the long silence. "You want to know something, Joey. I don't think we will ever see Grandpa Lane alive again. I think he is ready to die."

Joey muttered, "Maybe you're right." Joey

didn't want to talk about it with his sister. He didn't even want to think about it. But he knew that the day he was dreading so much, the day when his grandpa would die, was getting so close.

# 7

## GOODBYE, GRANDPA

Joey was almost home from school when he noticed the car in the garage. Something had to be wrong! "What's mom doing home from work now?" he wondered.

As soon as he entered the house he knew what was wrong. His mother's eyes were red from crying. Jennifer was wiping her eyes.

"It's grandpa," said Mrs. Andrews. "He died about two o'clock."

Joey rushed and threw his arms around his mother. He had known that this day was coming. Still, he didn't know what to say or do. As he hugged his mom, tears trickled down his cheeks.

Finally, he said, "I am going to miss him so much, mom. He was so great."

"I know," she replied. "We are all going to miss him. I am just so thankful that I still have the two of you."

Mrs. Andrews sat down on the living room sofa. Jennifer sat on one side of her. Joey sat on the other side. He felt strangely like a little child who wanted to be very close to his mother.

"What happened to grandpa?" Joey asked.

"Miss Kinney called me at work from the nursing home," said his mom. "She said that grandpa had slept all morning. Then, when she went to check him this afternoon, he had died. He just fell asleep. I guess Mr. Slater was sitting right there reading, and he didn't even realize anything had happened to grandpa."

Tears started to build up in Karen Andrews' eyes again. "Don't worry, mom," said Jennifer. "Joey and I will take care of you now."

"Sure, we told grandpa that we will help you," Joey added.

Their mom smiled. "When did you talk to grandpa about taking care of me?" she asked.

"Yesterday," said Joey. "He talked all about death. He talked about life too."

Jennifer and Joey told their mother all about the things that Grandpa Lane had told them the day before.

After hearing what grandpa had said, their mother spoke. "Maybe God answered our prayers by giving grandpa a strong faith and some real confidence as his death came near." Her tears had vanished. "I am so happy to know that grandpa told you those things. He was so good and loving. I hope you can both grow up to be like him."

Jennifer said, "We will try to be like he asked us to be."

"We are going to miss him though, aren't we?" said Joey.

"Yes, we are," answered their mom, "especially for a while."

She gave them each another squeeze. Then she jumped up and said, "But now there are many things for us to do. I will have to call your Uncle Jeff first to tell him what has happened. Then, when he gets here, we will have to make plans for the funeral."

"When is the funeral?" asked Joey.

"What day is it today?" asked Mrs. Andrews. "I can't even think very straight right now."

"Wednesday," said Jennifer.

"It will probably be on Saturday then," she replied. "Before that, though, there is so much to do. I will have to take some time off from work. We will have to make plans at the funeral home and at the church. I haven't even called Pastor Don yet. There will be so many plans to make and so many people to call."

"Don't worry about it, mom," said Jennifer reassuringly. "We will help you."

"Sure," added Joey, as his mother went to the phone in the kitchen to call Uncle Jeff.

Almost two days passed. Many plans and arrangements were made.

It was Friday morning. Jennifer and Joey had stayed home from school and were sitting in the family room. They were waiting for their mother and Uncle Jeff and Aunt Chris. The five of them were scheduled to be at the funeral home at ten o'clock to see Grandpa Lane's body. Joey was trying to read a new baseball magazine, but he wasn't doing well. He couldn't keep his mind on what he was reading.

"Jenn, have you ever seen a dead person?" he asked.

"No," answered Jennifer quietly.

"Are you worried about going to see grandpa?" asked Joey.

Jennifer said, "Not really."

"I am afraid," said Joey. "I wouldn't even go along if mom didn't make me go. I don't know what grandpa will look like. I don't know what I will do or how I'll act when we get there."

"You will be okay," Jennifer reassured him.

"I don't know." Joey wasn't so confident. "I don't like sickness and death. You know how I didn't want to go to the nursing home at first. Jenn, I was so scared when we went to see grandpa that first time. I even hid in that dumb shed

to stay away on Christmas Eve. Now, I'm afraid
again. What can I do?" Joey usually did not talk
so honestly and so seriously with his sister.

"You have to go," Jennifer said. "I'll stick with
you. We will be all right."

Their mother came down the stairs. "Let's go,"
she said. "You will need your jackets. Get them
on. Jeff and Chris will be right down."

Joey looked at Jennifer. Their discussion was
over. He was glad that she would be there even
though he didn't tell her that.

Joey felt cold and nervous as they entered
the funeral home. He could hear music playing
softly. He and Jenn each held one of their mother's hands as they entered the room where grandpa's body was lying in a casket. There were
bouquets of flowers on each side of the casket.
Joey's mom, Uncle Jeff and Aunt Chris all started
to cry a little when they saw grandpa's body.
Joey's mom cried hard. She buried her face in
her hands as she sobbed.

Joey looked at Grandpa Lane's body. It wasn't
as scary and difficult as he had expected. He
could only see grandpa's body from the waist
up. Half of the casket was closed. Mr. Warren,
the funeral director, had put grandpa's blue suit
on him. Grandpa was wearing a white shirt and
a red and blue striped tie. His gray hair was

neatly combed, just the way grandpa always kept it combed.

Mrs. Andrews walked to where her brother and his wife were standing. Uncle Jeff put his arm around his sister and whispered something that Joey did not hear. Aunt Chris also spoke to her in very hushed tones. After a little while, the three of them wiped their eyes and walked around and looked at the flowers. Many of the flowers had been sent by friends.

Jennifer whispered to Joey. "He looks better now than when we saw him at the nursing home on Tuesday." She looked at her grandpa a little longer and said, "He looks just like he is sleeping, doesn't he."

"His face is a different color, though," said Joey quietly. "It looks so much darker than it was."

"What are you two talking about so quietly?" asked their mother as she came and stood behind them.

"I think grandpa's face looks a different color than it was," answered Joey. "His face was so white before he died. Now he looks so much darker."

"Mr. Warren put a kind of make-up on grandpa's face as he got his body ready to be buried," she explained. "That is what makes the color look a little different."

"I think he looks good," said Jennifer.

"I guess I think so too," said Joey. "You know something. Death doesn't scare me so much after thinking about what grandpa told us on Tuesday."

"I'm glad." Mrs. Andrews was smiling again. "I'm glad for our faith and for the fact that we don't have to be afraid."

Mr. Warren came into the room and gave a little folder to each of them. Each folder had a picture of Jesus on the outside. On the inside was the Twenty-third Psalm on one side. On the other side was information about Grandpa Lane. It told when he was born and when he died. It also had information about the funeral. Everyone who came to the funeral to see Grandpa Lane's body would get one of these folders.

They stayed at the funeral home for almost an hour. They talked to Mr. Warren about some details for the funeral. They talked about grandpa and recalled a few old memories about him. As they were leaving the funeral home, Joey pulled Jennifer quietly over to one side and said, "Hey Jenn, this wasn't nearly as bad as I expected it to be."

"I told you everything would be all right," she said with a smile.

Joey returned the smile. It was a smile that

expressed relief, a smile that reflected a kind of victory.

The funeral service was held at the church at one-thirty on Saturday afternoon.

The church was almost full when Joey and Jennifer, along with their mom and Uncle Jeff and Aunt Chris, were ushered to the front pew. Seeing the closed casket at the front of the church made Joey feel very sad. He found himself crying as he sat down. So was everyone else in the front pew.

During the service, they sang some familiar hymns. Pastor Don read some parts of the Bible that told about God's love. They prayed. In his sermon, Pastor Don did not say very much about grandpa. He did talk about grandpa's faith in Jesus though. He talked more about God's promises for those who trust in Jesus. The words that meant the most to Joey were words that Pastor Don quoted from the Bible saying that "nothing can separate us from the love of God." Not even death!

When the service was over, six of grandpa's friends carried the casket out of the church to the hearse. That was another hard part. Again, Joey found some tears sneaking out.

He felt better when they got into Uncle Jeff's car. Most of the people who were in church got into cars. They followed the hearse to the cemetery where Grandpa Lane would be buried.

Lakeside Cemetery was on the edge of Forestburg, near a little lake. Joey noticed that the water of the lake was a sparkling blue as the warm April sunshine reflected off it.

The casket was carried to a small frame, which had been placed over the open grave. Joey knew that the grave was right next to Grandma Lane's grave. He had come out to the cemetery with grandpa many times to put flowers on her grave. The casket was set in place on the frame.

Everyone moved in close to the place where the casket was. Pastor Don read some words about Jesus' victory over death. As he read, he threw a little dirt on top of the casket. The short service at the cemetery ended with a prayer.

Many people stopped to shake hands with Joey's mom and Uncle Jeff before leaving the cemetery. Joey stood off to one side and watched his mother.

Pastor Don stopped to talk to Joey. He said, "I'm proud of you, Joey. You brought your grandfather so much happiness with your visits to the nursing home. He told me so."

Joey wasn't sure what he should say. He finally said, "Thanks," and gave the pastor a bashful smile.

"I'm sure Mr. Slater is going to miss Grandpa

Lane," Pastor Don added. "He liked your grandpa a lot. He enjoyed you and Jennifer too. Maybe you can still stop and visit with Mr. Slater once in awhile."

"I will," said Joey. "I like Mr. Slater, and I know he likes to have visitors."

"Good." Pastor Don gently slapped Joey on the shoulder as he left.

As Joey stood alone, he felt a mixture of sadness and joy. He knew he would miss Grandpa Lane. But the sunshine, the singing of the birds, the sparkling blue water of the lake, and the soft wind blowing through the many trees at the cemetery all were like reminders of God's love that never ends. Joey thought about those words, "Nothing can separate us from the love of God."

Joey looked again at the casket which would soon be lowered into the ground. "Goodbye, Grandpa Lane," he whispered. He had to wipe a few more tears from his eyes.

He realized that Jennifer was standing beside him. "Come on, Jenn," he said. "Grandpa is okay, and we have things to do."

"Sure," said Jennifer. "Mom needs us now, and she will need us more when Uncle Jeff goes back to his home."

As they walked toward Uncle Jeff's car, Joey added excitedly, "Mr. Slater is still going to need us too. And so will Mrs. Simon and Mrs. Duncan."

"There are probably all kinds of people that need us," said Jennifer.

Karen Andrews caught up with Joey and his sister. She put an arm around each of her children. They all smiled at each other. Then, together they walked to the car.